THIS IS ME
I AM...

A JOURNEY OF SELF-DISCOVERY

Edited By Briony Kearney

First published in Great Britain in 2024 by:

Young Writers® —— Est. 1991 —

Young Writers
Remus House
Coltsfoot Drive
Peterborough
PE2 9BF
Telephone: 01733 890066
Website: www.youngwriters.co.uk

All Rights Reserved
Book Design by Ashley Janson
© Copyright Contributors 2023
Softback ISBN 978-1-83565-171-1

Printed and bound in the UK by BookPrintingUK
Website: www.bookprintinguk.com
YB0579B

AMBITIOUS
OPTIMISTIC
LONELY
CREATIVE
KIND
PROUD
ANGRY
SHY HAPPY
LOYAL ANXIOUS
PASSIONATE
CONFIDENT
STRONG
ADVENTUROUS
BRAVE BORED
FEARLESS
SENSITIVE
EXTROVERTED
INTROVERTED
SAD STRESSED
AFRAID
MISUNDERSTOOD
FRUSTRATED

FOREWORD

Since 1991, here at Young Writers we have celebrated the awesome power of creative writing, especially in young adults where it can serve as a vital method of expressing their emotions and views about the world around them. In every poem we see the effort and thought that each student published in this book has put into their work and by creating this anthology we hope to encourage them further with the ultimate goal of sparking a life-long love of writing.

Our latest competition for secondary school students, This Is Me: I Am..., challenged young writers to write about themselves, considering what makes them unique and expressing themselves freely and honestly, something which is so important for these young adults to feel confident and listened to. There were no restrictions on style or subject so you will find an anthology brimming with a variety of poetic styles and topics. We hope you find it as absorbing as we have.

We encourage young writers to express themselves and address subjects that matter to them, which sometimes means writing about sensitive or contentious topics. If you have been affected by any issues raised in this book, details on where to find help can be found at www.youngwriters.co.uk/info/other/contact-lines

CONTENTS

Independent Entrants

Rhys Manser (17)   1

ACS International School, Cobham

Sora Fukushima (12)   2
Coco Assa (11)   4
Ava Robson (14)   5

Astor Secondary School, Dover

Georgie Morris (15)   6

Aurora Hedgeway School, Pilning

Oliver Fry (13)   8
Castiel Harris (13)   10
Austin Allen (14)   11
Leah Bufton (11)   12
James Moore (11)   13
Sam Castle (12)   14
Lacey Godwin (13)   15
Douglas Chandler (13)   16
Leo James (16)   17
Jack Smart (14)   18
Kenzo Sidonio (13)   19

Benenden School, Benenden

Anika Malik (13)   20
Kristen Wong (13)   21

Bluecoat Wollaton Academy, Wollaton Park

Gabrielle Smith-Strachan (14)   22

Chertsey High School, Addlestone

Jakob Worrall (13)   23
Frazer Rose   24

Crickhowell High School, Crickhowell

Thomas Slocombe (12)   25
Rose Jackson (13)   26
Eve Powell (14)   28
Gracie Jackson (13)   30
William MacDonald (14)   31

Dyson Perrins CE Academy, Malvern

Alexis Carroll (11)   32
Evan Lawrence (11)   34

Elfrida Rathbone Camden - Leighton Education Project, London

Khyle Mangal (19)   35
Ayobami Odumosu (16)   36
Tyrone Forde (18)   38
Shem Simon (18)   40
Chelsea Bradley   42

Gosforth Academy, Gosforth

Ben Robinson	43

Heolddu Comprehensive School, Bargoed

Brooklynn Dobbs (17)	44
Mason Jones (13)	46
Julia Hamod (13)	47
Freya (13)	48
Bethan Cluer (13)	49
Ethan Owen (12)	50
Jackson Payne (10)	51
Kian Duggan (13)	52
Isabelle Bir (11)	53
Kodi Thomas (12)	54
Hollie James-Baker (13)	55
Rachel Davies (13)	56
Kacie Price (13)	57
Rhys Wood (14)	58
Megan Stedman (13)	59
Evan Browne (14)	60
Isabella Williams (11)	61
Aaron Mcvey (13)	62
Sophie James (13)	63
Thomas Chard (14)	64
Kody Price (12)	65
Ethanjay Harding (11)	66
Alfie Cusack	67
Dewi Miles (12)	68
George Holdsworth (13)	69
Niamh Higgs (11)	70
Sophie Evans (12)	71
Zak Pearson (11)	72
Blake Price (14)	73
Gethin Evesham (12)	74
Summer Ellis (11)	75
Megan James (11)	76
Ben Watkins (12)	77
Lexie Derraven (12)	78
Alfie Hollifield (13)	79
Jenson Griffiths (11)	80
Lloyd Smith (11)	81
Chloe Evans (11)	82
Peyton John (13)	83
Reegan Thomas (11)	84
Coen Jones (14)	85
Lola Heath (12)	86
Gracie Jenkins (12)	87
Matthew Heywood (12)	88
Oliver Stedman (11)	89
Kian Hurley (13)	90
Jake Thomas (12)	91
Phoebe Underwood (12)	92
Aimee Thomas (12)	93
Callum Charles (14)	94
Jesse Lewis (12)	95
Reuben Smith (12)	96
Lucas Tamcken (14)	97
Alfie Jones (13)	98
Sarah Banks	99
Emily Zhu (13)	100
Lexi-Joanne McMahon (12)	101
Ava Williams (13)	102
Lexie Pascoe (10)	103
Maisie Harrison (14)	104
Allise Yuile (11)	105
Evie Carver (11)	106
Harry Allison (10)	107
Niamh Eynon (12)	108
Neve O'Callaghan (11)	109
Connor James (10)	110
Lloyd James (12)	111
George Hamod (11)	112
Willow Farrell (11)	113
Kian Christensen (12)	114
Jacob Davies (11)	115
Lily Gardner (13)	116
Kaylyn Woodward (12)	117

John Willmott School, Sutton Coldfield

Ire Ajimuda (16)	118
Dylan Trowman (16)	120
Quayumm Oluwa (16)	121
Melissa Hayden (15)	122

Kimbolton School, Kimbolton

Eloise King (14)	123
Poppy Todd Boutou (13)	125

La Retraite RC Girls' School, Clapham Park

Amina Benzait (11)	127
Pison Mulugeta (12)	128
Imaan Javid (11)	130
Nila Connors (11)	132
Hosanna Samson (11)	134
Kaira-Siti Hawley (11)	136
Hannah Odeh (11)	138
Des'shaniea Stephenson-King (11)	140
Mitcheka Jackson (11)	141
Elyona Adonis Opoku (12)	142
Jessica-Ria Miyanda (11)	143
Maria Iloba (12)	144
Penelope Aubrey Sales (11)	145
Aicha Cisse (11)	146
Christianah Ajanaku (11)	147
Temidire Adejuwon (11)	148
Eguono Ehwenomare (11)	149

New College Pontefract, Pontefract

Nevaeh Kwan (17)	150
Kimberley Eglen (16)	153
Lilian Fanthorpe (16)	154
Belle Needham (17)	156
Kairos Ford (17)	158
Jasmine Gibson (16)	160
Harriet Marris (16)	161
Aimee Smith (16)	162

Seadown School, Worthing

Jake Offord (14)	163
Josh Willis (14)	164
Faye Bowles (12)	165
Kai Jardine (16)	166
Jonty (7)	167

The Commonweal School, Swindon

Keshav Bansal (12)	168
Bekah Ashdown (12)	169
Ariadne Uphill	170
Georgina Mercer (12)	171
Evie Wischhusen (11)	172
Lola Alderson (12)	173
Christina Paterson (12)	174
Emily Pidduck	175
Alice Poole (11)	176

DIFFERENT RELAXED FUN LONELY
STRONG FIERCE POSITIVE
OPTIMISTIC ADVENTUROUS
PASSIONATE HAPPY
ANXIOUS

THE POEMS

EXTROVERTED STRESSED
FEARLESS AMBITIOUS
LOYAL ANGRY
MISUNDERSTOOD OK PROUD
GRATEFUL FINE
TOUGH
BORED
SAD
WISE
STRONG CHILL INTROVERTED
BRAVE ENERGETIC
KIND
UPBEAT WISE TRUSTWORTHY
QUIET

THIS IS ME: I AM - A JOURNEY OF SELF-DISCOVERY

Mr R

My name is Rishi
I am the Prime Minister
My job's important
Only if I do it right
I may rarely do that, but
It's the thought that counts.

Rhys Manser (17)

The White Blanket

The sky is clear and bright, the weather is perfect,
the bright sun shines onto the white snow,
making everything look like a picture.
Through my window, I see elegant snowflakes
drifting down to the ground.
My garden looks like it was covered
in an ironed white blanket,
not a single mistake is left behind.
The ugly dried brown grass is gone,
and not a single coloured leaf is left behind,
making all the trees look naked
without their brown leaves.
The bare branches balance snow on their arms
while the subtle wind shakes the extra snow to the floor.
Before I know what's happening,
I'm downstairs, putting my jacket and boots on.
I walk outside and drop myself into the snow,
I can feel myself slowly sinking
into the thick snow,
my dark skin clashes with the white snow
making the snow look unrealistic.
After a while, I'm submerged in snow,
slowly, the snow starts turning more comforting and safe,
reminding me of a white blanket embracing me.
The snow covers my body,

covering all my insecurities and mistakes,
making me feel protected.
It felt nice, for once, no one judged me,
the snow momentarily shields me from reality.
After a while, my mother calls me to come back in.
The moment I hear her voice,
I am instantly jolted back to reality,
I slowly get up and brush the snow off my body,
uncovering what I wish would stay covered.
Now I'm out of the snow
with no white blanket to protect me
from those who judge me from my past.

Sora Fukushima (12)
ACS International School, Cobham

My Powerful Poem!

My life is like a butterfly, flying through the sky,
flapping its wings to the beat of a drum.
Like its attributes to the world, to Mother Earth,
to a tiny flower, and even its beauty is a gift.
I feel as if I could fly up to the sky
just to see its beautiful wonders!
To feel the cool wind touch my skin,
for the warmth of a cloud to comfort me.
As my tears fall from my face
as if they were rain droplets
falling from a lonely cloud in the sky.
For it is only nature
that can encourage me to go further.
To breathe in the sweet air
and feel the soft colourful grass that is full of life.
Is life a lesson or a blessing?
A meaning or feeling,
it almost feels like a critic
or maybe even a supporter.
Nobody knows and will they ever?

Coco Assa (11)
ACS International School, Cobham

Floating

The whole world fades,
it disappears in a blink.
No matter how many times I smile and wink,
the runny tears come.
It's sunny outside,
but inside me is a storm.
I want to scream and shout.
Please, let me let it all out.
All my stress, all my worries.
I hate being in a dress.
I want to wear something baggy
to cover up all my flesh.
Bless little me,
who was so tiny and vulnerable.
I was so loveable.
I love myself,
above my heart is nothing but sadness,
corrupting me as icky
Tears, tears, tears keep coming.
I'm in the bathroom stall,
I walk out and put on my bloody mask.
And I repeat, repeat, repeat, for 230 more days
until summer break.
Then I will float.

Ava Robson (14)
ACS International School, Cobham

A Thank You

All my life, I was told there was some prince out there for me,
I always dreamed of my one and only,
Of my husband-to-be.
As I grew, I had a number of princes,
None of them true,
None of them you.
You were my Prince Charming.
You pulled me out of the darkness,
You pulled me from my worst self.
You were it.
We'd plan our home,
Our children,
Our lives,
Together.
I thought it was true.
I believed the lie that people really grow old together,
That people stayed together forever.
I hated you,
I had so much anger because you left,
You were my glue.

Our chapter ended a while ago,
I now realise that you were in my life for a reason,
You were here to show me what love is,
What happiness is,

As much as I hate you for pushing me back into the darkness,
I thank you for showing me that I can come out of it.
That I can be happy,
That I can be loved.
Thank you.

Georgie Morris (15)
Astor Secondary School, Dover

My Name Is Oliver

My name is Oliver,
I like cars,
Primarily Fords,

My dream is to be a mechanic
Who works with Fords,

And to own
A Bullitt Mustang,

Problem is,
Not many were made for the UK!

I also like Mondeos,
Except the last ones are 2022s!

Not just that,
But I also like F150s!

And these aren't even made for the UK,
They're all imported from the USA!

And I don't just like cars and pickups,
I like buses too!

I love an ADL Enviro200,
Especially an Enviro300 City CBG!

I also like a nice double-deck Enviro MMC!

And here's the end,
And what makes me Oliver!

Oliver Fry (13)
Aurora Hedgeway School, Pilning

All About Myths And Legends

I like reading about Ancient Egypt and dragons,
My favourite God is Anubis, son of Set.
I like how dragons fly sky-high, soaring through the clouds.
I like how Anubis has a jackal's head and people believe he takes the people through a safe passage to the next world.
I like dragons but the ones I like most are the ones who have their horns swirly.
When learning about the other gods, I snore.
I like how Egyptians prepare for the next world.
This is all about my favourite myths by Castiel Matthew Haden Harris.

Castiel Harris (13)
Aurora Hedgeway School, Pilning

My Stunning Trip To Lanzarote

I landed in Spain, sunny Spain,
The weather was hot, oh so hot,
We got on a bus,
It went from hot to cold with the AC,
Looked rich, lucky rich,
We looked around, around and around,
I could swear I was in Heaven, felt like Heaven,
So much there to do, we did it all,
We adventured and found food,
Steak, juicy steak, yummy steak,
We had to go back,
But booked a trip, a volcanic trip,
It was so fun,
It came to tea time, we had food,
We got back on a plane to play in the rain.

Austin Allen (14)
Aurora Hedgeway School, Pilning

Me

I have a schnauzer,
he is a wowzer.
I like my cat,
she sleeps on a mat.
I like dragons,
they carry wagons.
I like birds,
they travel in herds.
I like food,
it puts me in a good mood.
I like the colour blue,
I'd like to have blue glue...
I love chips,
put them in dips.
I have tablet time, but only for an hour,
it's like it gives me power.

Leah Bufton (11)
Aurora Hedgeway School, Pilning

Intelligent

- **I** am James
- **N** eed some help?
- **T** ry to guess my favourite football club
- **E** asy?
- **L** ike this will be too
- **L** ines are straight, circles are round
- **I** don't know about triangles
- **G** et some shapes
- **E** xtra riddles?
- **N** o need to worry unless you want
- **T** o have less because I will bless.

James Moore (11)
Aurora Hedgeway School, Pilning

Sam's Emotions And Hobbies

My emotions are different,
I am sometimes sad, angry, happy, scared or even frustrated.
But I always try to be happy.
I have all sorts of hobbies,
I like TV, Oculus, PlayStation and playing outside.
But I struggle sometimes to listen.
I am allowed to feel how I feel.

Sam Castle (12)
Aurora Hedgeway School, Pilning

I Am My Best Friend

- **G** orgeous girl
- **E** ntertaining with laughter
- **O** utstanding talents
- **R** omantic and flirtatious
- **G** ifted with super energy
- **I** ncredibly patient
- **A** nnoying but the best!

Lacey Godwin (13)
Aurora Hedgeway School, Pilning

Dougie

D id you know that
O ctober is the spookiest month?
U p
G oat is nice
I like video games
E veryone at my school are fools.

Douglas Chandler (13)
Aurora Hedgeway School, Pilning

I Love My Dog Haiku

I love my cute dogs,
They are two cocker spaniels,
Albie and Rufus.

They are so playful,
They love to go on big walks,
Then they eat some food.

Leo James (16)
Aurora Hedgeway School, Pilning

My Acrostic

J umping from trees
A bsolutely loves hot sauce
C atching bugs
K icking people

This is me.

Jack Smart (14)
Aurora Hedgeway School, Pilning

The Stranger

Spends his time walking,
Why he does this,
I don't know,
Maybe he is mad.

Kenzo Sidonio (13)
Aurora Hedgeway School, Pilning

The Sun Shines

The sun shines on the world and makes the people smile,
The sun makes the crops grow and the laundry dry.

Sometimes, the sun doesn't shine on the world and doesn't make the people smile,
It tries and tries but just doesn't shine.

Other times, the sun disappears from sight,
It hides behind the clouds and the people don't smile,
The sun cries and cries but nothing is wrong.

Some days, the sun shines too brightly and sets fire to the fields,
The people don't smile, they cry
Because it's just too dry.

Just
Like
Me.

But every sun sometimes doesn't shine,
And every sun has times when it hides behind the clouds,
And every sun shines too brightly sometimes.

Just
Like
Us.

Anika Malik (13)
Benenden School, Benenden

What Am I?

I am the rising wisps of one weak wish,
I am the wind that blows between your lips,
I am the mouth of the bottle you kissed,
I am your words, thoughts, and undying itch.

I take shade under a cherry on top,
I live in the ink from which shot stars drop,
I reflect in the penny of a well,
I ride the boat where from the shore it sails.

I am not physical, nor present, do not be misled,
I loom by your head, your smile, your heart, whatever you've said,
I was your moon, your stars, your bothersome burden back then.
I am not sorry that you will never find me again.

You could try, but you'll never raise the dead.

Kristen Wong (13)
Benenden School, Benenden

I Am

Daily affirmations are an effective way to encourage yourself, but they aren't always as effective as people say
But I'll just forget that part, anyway
I am smart, but I get so many things wrong
I am fearless, yet I am afraid
I am beautiful, but I can't look in the mirror without seeing a flaw
I am perfect, but I have scars

I am strong, but I falter
I am loved, even still, people hate me
I am powerful, but my words don't matter
I am enough, but I always feel battered

It's one thing to tell yourself this, but do you really believe?
It's hard to turn a blind eye to the things people say
Maybe if I try to forget I will do well
All you have to do is come out of your shell

You can continue to look around you and watch others reach their dream
But it's not always as good as it seems
If I just focus on being me
Maybe I will finally succeed.

Gabrielle Smith-Strachan (14)
Bluecoat Wollaton Academy, Wollaton Park

The Rock

There was a rock that stood on the side of the road,
That rock then continued to slowly roll to the end,
But in the end, it never made it and
The rock rolled off the road
And into a river, that rock then slowly sank to the bottom
And continued to roll under the water,
And the rock rolled and rolled
Until it found itself
In the ocean, where it was washed up by fish and animals,
At the end of its adventurous life, it rolled all the way to the beach.

Jakob Worrall (13)
Chertsey High School, Addlestone

This Is Me

These are the bricks that built me,
Computing, programming, OnePlus.
Started from the bottom,
Building up to the top.

Spending my life sat down,
Never far from a screen.
Ruining my eyesight,
But in my eyes, it's a dream.

Frazer Rose
Chertsey High School, Addlestone

Nerdy, Different, Weird

Weird, what about passionate?
Nerdy, what about curious and hardworking?
Different, without diversity, life is bland.

People with these amazing qualities are neglected, mistreated and sometimes even abused,
We're constantly giving up our time being 'nerdy' and 'weird',
We're making ourselves interesting, hardworking and passionate individuals,
After the teenage years end, those abusers are lost, and we flourish,
We're investing our time, making the world know about our passion,
Making them know that we want to make a difference,
Making them know that we're different,
And that's not always a bad thing.

Thomas Slocombe (12)
Crickhowell High School, Crickhowell

Sticks And Stones May Break My Bones

I stared into the mirror and I saw me standing there,
I didn't wear make-up and I didn't care.
I stood a little shorter, my hair was a bright frizzy red,
But I didn't notice until somebody said.

They peered at me closely, like vultures circling around,
I said they didn't hurt me, but their words tackled me to the ground.
The next day I stood there, my eyes a bloodshot red,
Their nasty words were like a virus infecting my head.

Every day I got stronger, eventually I let them go,
But doubt held more power, and those nasty thoughts would poke.
My complexion was pale (but you can blame my hair),
I have loads of bumps and lumps scattered everywhere.

Then I looked again, and I realised I was being meek,
I am nowhere near ugly, no, I am just unique.
So, anyone out there who thinks that they are not worth it,
You should own being different, no one is perfect.

I now wear those insults on my shoulders like a medal,
Although they cut and bruise me, they show me that I am special.

And those people who feel insecure and want to make a fuss,
I am better off not listening because they're probably just jealous.

So, I'll look in the mirror again and what do I see?
I see my imperfections, but they make me, *me*.

Rose Jackson (13)
Crickhowell High School, Crickhowell

Butterflies Can't See Their Wings

"*Butterflies can't see their wings.*"
I stare and I stare,
But all that I see
Is a version of me
That I don't want to be.
My reflection is honest,
Brutal and true.
Maybe all I need
Is a different view.

"*They can't see how truly beautiful they are.*"
Everywhere I look,
All that I see
Are beautiful people
That I wish could be me.
My eyes brown,
My hair a mess.
Why do I have to look
So much less?

"*But everyone else can.*"
I wish that I had
Her eyes or her nose,
And all of her

Bright and colourful clothes.
It seems unfair to me,
That only I can't have
True beauty.

"People are like that as well."
I compare myself to them,
They compare themselves to me.
This cycle needs to stop
And I definitely agree,
There is no point in complaining
About how you were born to be.
There's supposed to be a difference between you and me,
And that's something that everyone needs to see.

"Butterflies can't see their wings.
They can't see how truly beautiful they are,
But everyone else can.
People are like that as well."

Eve Powell (14)
Crickhowell High School, Crickhowell

Enough

I am not like other girls,
I am not a clone,
I will *not* be made up for society,
While judgment sits on a throne.

I am not like other girls,
I don't need to have thin thighs,
I don't *want* to be good enough,
If my happiness is the price.

I am not some playdough,
Wanting to be shaped,
I don't want to weigh in feathers,
Unless I want to break.

Gracie Jackson (13)
Crickhowell High School, Crickhowell

Beneath The Surface

I am me,
But that's not what other people see.
I am clouded with misconceptions,
Untruthful, false perceptions.

What I am is joy,
Like a child playing with a toy.
I am full of passion,
For that is my fashion.

My mind is vibrant with inspiration,
I just struggle with the communication.
My character once remained concealed
But now it has been revealed.

William MacDonald (14)
Crickhowell High School, Crickhowell

Meet Me

If you really want to know me,
Warning: there is more than the eye can see,
To my favourite goddess in Greek mythology,
And to why my favourite subject isn't technology.
I love to be in photos,
And I even have my own motto:
"In order to insult me, I must first value your opinion. Nice try though."

Did you know I'm dyslexic?
And the only thing that relates to me that rhymes is my name, Alexis.
People call me sassy,
When I daydream, I am never classy.

I have two cats,
I don't really wear hats.
I love English, drawing and Maths,
And to get there, I walk the same paths.
I'm not really scared of ghosts,
And I hate people who boast.

As I wrote this, I was listening to 'Say My Name' from Beetlejuice.
My favourite goddess is the daughter of Zeus.
Though, that doesn't really help does it?

Well, I got you in my mitts.
It's Athena, couldn't you tell?

Just this morning, I told my friends:
"You can say, 'Have a nice day,' without a problem,
But you cannot say, 'Enjoy the next 24 hours,'
Without sounding remotely threatening."
So I warn you,
There is more to me than you previously knew.

I love music, art, and drama,
I really believe in karma.
People may say I'm rude,
But I give them the death stare and they know that they're doomed.

So, that's all about me (almost),
Just remember, I'm not what you see,
Don't let my blonde hair fool you,
Because there's more to this girl than you knew,
I'm smarter and wiser than the person who made the legend,
And I want to help that to be amended.

'Cause as far as I'm concerned,
I'm gonna do Athena proud.

Alexis Carroll (11)
Dyson Perrins CE Academy, Malvern

Most Needed Things

F ootball
A crostic poems
M um
I am unique
L ove
Y ou are unique.

Evan Lawrence (11)
Dyson Perrins CE Academy, Malvern

This Is Me

My dog's name is Jake,
I like brown Mr Kipling cakes.

My favourite films are 'All Dogs Go To Heaven'
And 'Toy Story 3',
This is me and I like to be free.

Arsenal is my football team,
Vanilla is my favourite ice cream.

I have a long beard that's shiny and black,
I like to watch the train on the tracks.

I like a beating drum,
And having fun.

I like Nando's, roast chicken to be exact,
I enjoy to speak about facts.

Gardening is my passion,
And I love fashion.

Staring is rude and not a joke,
I like to dance to the English folk.

At my core, you will find,
A big beating heart
That's one of a kind.

Khyle Mangal (19)
Elfrida Rathbone Camden - Leighton Education Project, London

This Is Me

This is me Ayo Odumosu
I'm awesome kind and bold.
I've got a heart of gold.
I love, love.
I love drawing and I don't think it's boring.
Being an animator is my ultimate core
Or a YouTuber.
I love my parents and I love my sister and there are none before misters.
My favourite food is spaghetti and I love an awesome party.
I'm always happy and it's not too shabby.
Drawing is my favourite hobby and I do it non-stoppy.
My characters I made up are the awesome team and they are living the dream.
My main three favourite TV shows are 'Thomas & Friends', 'The Loud House' and 'My Little Pony: Friendship is Magic'
And my life is not really tragic.
My favourite colour is awesome blue and it's too good to be true.
I was born in 2007 and to me it's all heaven.
My favourite animal is a baby harp seal and it's no big deal.
My favourite movies are 'Thomas & Friends', 'Cars 2' and 'PAW Patrol TMovie'
Music makes me groovy.
My favourite restaurants are McDonald's and Cosmos and I love hot chocolate with marshmallows.

3 to the 1 to the 1 to the 3, I'm awesome as you can see.
My favourite place is Butlin's and I'm here for the wins.
I like all my friends and drawing is my favourite hobby to no ends...

Ayobami Odumosu (16)
Elfrida Rathbone Camden - Leighton Education Project, London

This Is Me

This is me, I am Tyrone.
When I leave Colly, I would like to, I don't know.
You might find me in JD making that p.
I am made of jerk chicken, mac and cheese, curry goat, bun and cheese.

At my core, you will find me,
Standing at 5'11, brown eyes, black hair, no one can compare.
I like fashion, that's my passion.
I got one ear piercing, you see it glistening,
It shines like a shooting star, reaching far.
People think I'm a cheater, no I'm a thrill-seeker.
Strong, fearless, creative,
People, just stop hating!

My walls appear thin, but they're not.
People think I'm cool, kind and funny.
You can try take advantage of me, that's not happening g.
My family are the closest to me, especially my mum, she's a real g.
My sister is annoying - that's no joke.

You will find me listening to music every day of the week,
It makes me feel free.
I like my food, some oxtail stew and chilling with my boo in my room.

People ask where I'm from,
I'm Caribbean, but born in the streets of London.

If you was to ask me what I detest, it would be fish and spiders.
Unfortunately, that's just me.
I'm Tyrone the master g.

Tyrone Forde (18)
Elfrida Rathbone Camden - Leighton Education Project, London

This Is Me

I am Shem
This is me
I like games and movies
I'm punctual
I dislike football.

My life is an open book
I love to look at the computer all day long
It is like breathing in air.

I am Shem
This is me
I am from Eritrea
I have one brother and one sister
My dad is my favourite person
He is as tall as a giraffe
And he often makes me laugh.

Being forced to do something I don't like makes me angry
But this is me
I have a beard, a moustache and curly hair
And people often stare.

I am 18 years old
This is me
I am adventurous
I wish to travel the world

America, Canada and Eritrea.

I am as brave as a roaring lion
I love to eat
Pizza, for me, is like heaven
This is me.

I was born in the UK
I don't speak other languages
But enjoy my cultural dishes:
Ziyini, Injera and Doro Wat
Beef stew, flatbread, and chicken stew
This is me.

Shem Simon (18)
Elfrida Rathbone Camden - Leighton Education Project, London

This Is Me

This is me
My nanny is the best
For that I am blessed
I like to watch YouTube for fun
For exercise I like to run
At my core you will find a character that's very bold
Singing and dancing is my passion
I am at my best when I am in action
I do not like pickles, spiders or rats.
Feel free to join me for a chat
I am full of warmth, happiness and laughter, that makes me one of a kind,
There will only be one of me you will find.

Chelsea Bradley
Elfrida Rathbone Camden - Leighton Education Project, London

This Is Me

Set in stone and lodged in past. This is me alone.
Happy and positive, never upset. This is the me that is known.
Alone, you see a demon, set to wallow and lose and fail,
'Cause no one dares listen to me and beg to hear my tale.

A lonesome cry and desperate cheer is long to be forgotten,
But build up people and spread the cheer and your message will be gotten.
Burn these bridges and act unfair, and your crowd will soon be gone,
'Cause these expectations of all these people sure do weigh a ton.

Me: alone and desperate, needing some cheer,
But talking and meeting and finding new people leaves me in utter fear,
And one comment, unnecessary and rude, leads me into dismay,
And I can't seem to find the words: I'm not okay.

So that's my story, through and through, and I still do,
Pretend to be someone I'm not, from start to end of day,
I wonder and worry all day about me and how I seem,
But really, all I need is someone on my team.

Ben Robinson
Gosforth Academy, Gosforth

Maunder

Maundering,
Dwindling footsteps, soaked in rain,
Through an endless night, a sullen forest,
A lone deer, lost in sonder.
The beating rain continues, the leaves fall, the seasons change,
I remain here, still,
Maundering.
My gait of languid nation,
Each step unsure of the next,
Unsure of the road that beckons, its true purpose.
And so I remain here, still,
Maundering.

Maundering,
Cascading thoughts weigh down my shoulders,
Tumultuous storm clouds, with eyes like daggers,
How they pierce my form,
And I am known.
Here, yet in my entirety, I remain, still,
Maundering.
A flower blooms, knowing not of its seed, spreading purpose.
And yet, nevertheless, children precede it each spring,

So perhaps, just for one moment,
In this twilight, the droning silence pulsating in my ears,
May I bloom too?
'Til then, here I remain, still,
Maundering.

Brooklynn Dobbs (17)
Heolddu Comprehensive School, Bargoed

This Is Me, I Am

I am an overthinker and my own biggest enemy.
I am a hoarder of Transformers, PlayStation controllers, money and Nerf guns, ready to fire at my sisters.
I have a weakness for cold and every single tickle technique.
I have incredibly bad luck and that comes to my gaming experience.
I am aware my face does not say it all.
I am smart in Maths and English.
I am a winter baby.
I am a gamer.
I am a ton of fun but I am an enthusiastic singer, I sing my butt off in the shower.
I am a Christmas boy, not a New Year's boy.
I am afraid of the dark and Shaynie's dark side.
I am stubborn as hell until my phone is taken off me.
I am going to be an uncle soon for my brother's son.
I am a good listener.
I am a younger brother and a future uncle.
I am working on perfecting my maths and gaming.
I am always planning for the future of my journey.

Mason Jones (13)
Heolddu Comprehensive School, Bargoed

This Is Me

I am sensitive and nervous
I can be broken with insults
And stitched back together
With empty compliments

I am anxious and shy
Lacking confidence
Going unnoticed is my greatest talent
Living my life, invisible and happy

I am thoughtful and quiet
I observe and think
Think about other people
And what they think

I am caring and a people-pleaser
I put others' wishes before my own
And prefer to do whatever they decide
Too scared to upset anyone in any way

I'm sensitive and nervous
I'm anxious and shy
I'm thoughtful and quiet
I'm caring and a people-pleaser
This is how I act
This is how I feel
This is me.

Julia Hamod (13)
Heolddu Comprehensive School, Bargoed

This Is Me!

F reya Davies is my name
R espect is key and it gets me where I want to be
E very day, I am proud to live in Wales
Y ou have your aims and I have mine, mine are to be financially stable and to have a family to come home to every day
A lso, family is the most important thing to me and I believe I wouldn't be where I want to be without it
D ance is more than a hobby and is what I want to do forever
A dventurous, achieving, accepting
V ery understanding, helpful and independent is who I am
I believe it is important to have a healthy lifestyle
E njoyable, exciting
S o I guess that's just me.

Freya (13)
Heolddu Comprehensive School, Bargoed

Who Needs New Anymore?

I look around at those around me,
Watching on their phones;
Discussing newest games and flying fancy drones.
They talk about robots and fancy new AI;
I look towards their items, and all I ask is "Why?"
I love my phone, it's true;
The games and phone calls too,
However, who needs phones when you've got the older clones?
A record with a player can handle music taste,
A DS or a GameBoy can keep you entertained.
A classic DVD can show you a great film,
A good old-fashioned landline can cut down on the bill.
There really is no need
For modern toys and gadgets.
If you've got the old stuff,
You already will have it.

Bethan Cluer (13)
Heolddu Comprehensive School, Bargoed

The Truth Of Rugby

Men going mad
Fighting like animals
For a funny-looking ball
To take it across a line.

Heads and shoulders
Bashing against one another
Battling it out in the open
Like wild beasts in battle.

Crooked noses
Broken bones
Clotted bruises
A devastating battle.

Watched and admired by people.

Up top, fierce beasts
Down below, fearless angry menaces
You try to defeat
Sometimes, it works
Other times, you fail.

This is rugby
We are not afraid
We fight
We defend
We are the WRU!

Ethan Owen (12)
Heolddu Comprehensive School, Bargoed

Big And Small

Small brain, big body
not a dog like Mr Peabody.
I'm really funny and not a bunny
Oh, and I need money!
My friend, Ethan, fell down the stairs
and screamed like Britney Spears,
nearly got put in a wheelchair.
He is very angry and stupid
when it comes to common sense,
but enough about Ethan,
the one who fell down the stairs,
and on to Harlee the nan slayer,
he is dumb like me!
But funny as can be,
so back on to Ethan,
he is funny but for some reason,
always blames his shoe!

Jackson Payne (10)
Heolddu Comprehensive School, Bargoed

I Am

I am Kian, a 13-year-old kid and this is me.
I love to ride motorbikes with my brothers and cousins.
I like roller coasters and thrills.
I love WWE, my favourite is John Cena and LA Knight.
I like pizza, my favourite topping is pepperoni - I don't like pineapple.
I like playing football and rugby with my cousin.
I hate spiders and snakes.
I like dogs.
I like going on family holidays.
I want to learn Welsh like my nan.
I like watching F1 and MotoGP with my dad, my favourite is Lewis Hamilton.

Kian Duggan (13)
Heolddu Comprehensive School, Bargoed

Dance Crazy!

This is me, I love dance
This is me, I dance my heart out on the floor
This is me, spending lots of hours in the studio trying to be the best that I can be.

This is me, dancing in a team
This is me, making memories of a lifetime
This is me, travelling around to many places.

This is me, dancing new routines
This is me, trying my best
This is me, trying to be the best that I can be!

This is me, sharing the floor with my team,
This is me, sharing memories with my friends!

Isabelle Bir (11)
Heolddu Comprehensive School, Bargoed

Football

F ootball is a wonderful sport, 22 players hoping to be the best
O nly one team can come on top in this awesome test
O n the pitch, everyone tries their best
T eams soar as fans chant to support the team they love
B est teams win and fans go home smiling
A ll of the passionate fans come together and chant
L eftbacks and brave defenders put their bodies on the line for their team
L ots of teams win and lots lose but that's fine.

Kodi Thomas (12)
Heolddu Comprehensive School, Bargoed

Dance Crazy

D ance is everything and all that you need
A ctive, non-stop, no matter what
N ever give up, even when it gets hard
C ontrol your body and stand up high
E ven when you feel like you're going to die!

C ontinuously learning new steps
R unning through my routines is what I do
A lways giving my all on the floor
Z one is what I get into before I dance
Y ou always need to give your best when you dance.

Hollie James-Baker (13)
Heolddu Comprehensive School, Bargoed

This Is Me

I am a mirror, I reflect light everywhere
I am a ray of sunshine, I spread selflessness
I am the patient hours, my forgiving diligence reminds me of who I am
I am a river, I flow effortlessly around rocks that get in my way
I am a book, I teach those around me
I am justice, I serve righteousness to those who deserve it
I am a flower in winter, my uniqueness will never compare
I am a tree stuck to its roots, no matter what force may come my way, my principles will never waver.

Rachel Davies (13)
Heolddu Comprehensive School, Bargoed

This Is Me

I am me,
A person who cannot think of the words,
My guitar says them for me,
So does my art.

I am me,
A person who is anxious about going out,
About being judged,
But I know the world is bigger than that,
The Earth, surrounded by stars in a solar system,
A solar system in a galaxy surrounded by galaxies.

So why do I worry so much?
Worry about being late to class,
About people's opinions,
I will never know.

Kacie Price (13)
Heolddu Comprehensive School, Bargoed

This Is Me!

Being among my mates, in that moment
With the ball in my hands is an escape from reality
When you step onto that field, everything, every problem just disappears
Your mates are beside you, fighting along
Seeing the scoreboard go up as you score
Your friends and teammates surrounding you, celebrating
If you get that far, maybe even lift a trophy
Now that is the best feeling you can get
Winning with your mates
That is the meaning of rugby!

Rhys Wood (14)
Heolddu Comprehensive School, Bargoed

This Is Me

T he love I get from my family makes me feel special
H appiness from buying my favourite things
I nventive minds during challenging times
S hopping keeps me busy for the day

I can distract myself with my phone when I'm upset
S ilence when I'm reading my favourite book

M eeting my cat for the first time made me friendlier to others
E veryone I know makes me feel welcome.

Megan Stedman (13)
Heolddu Comprehensive School, Bargoed

About Me

E verything has a need, a purpose, a job, from an ant to an elephant
V ertical photos help me see the planet's beauty and all there is to love
A ll things have beauty, cuteness and more, they need love and kindness, not to be murdered
N o animal deserves to just be killed and should be cared for and loved by people young and old
B eginnings don't start immediately, just remember this one and hold it by your heart.

Evan Browne (14)
Heolddu Comprehensive School, Bargoed

Overthinking

Inner thoughts invade, coming like a moth to a flame.
Heart racing in front of a crowd, as I try to reach my aim.
Despite all of this my mind will work, thinking, thinking, thinking.
Curiosity will demand for an answer, but hesitation reaches out, screaming, screaming, screaming.
The thoughts given to me, an overthinker, will cause my mind to sometimes overload.
So sometimes it is better to take a moment and allow my mind to go into a relaxation mode.

Isabella Williams (11)
Heolddu Comprehensive School, Bargoed

This Is Me

Football helps me cope
It also helps me hope
There's ups and downs
But mostly frowns
You can play on the left or right
Day and night
You will be alright
Because there is no fright
Football makes me happy
Like a baby in a nappy
With new toys to play
In football, you can be gay
Because in football, you can be free
And sometimes you might sit under a tree
And think to yourself, what a wonderful life to be.

Aaron Mcvey (13)
Heolddu Comprehensive School, Bargoed

Grew Up

I am older,
My once pink walls now snow-white.
My desk, which was once for drawing, now for make-up.
My princess dresses are now replaced with mini skirts.
My little doll heels were replaced with new and real heels.
Used to beg to stay up longer, but now I can't wait to sleep.
My once brown healthy hair is now dyed.
Once not caring about how you look, but now check every time you walk past a mirror.
I lost the little me, I grew up.

Sophie James (13)
Heolddu Comprehensive School, Bargoed

Happy

They say I'm fat and ugly,
They say I'm useless, a waste of space,
Others say I'm funny and kind,
Others say I'm talented and loyal,
They don't care for me,
They never will,
Others do,
Others lift me up and make me smile,
They ruin my day, my week, my year,
Others make my day, my week, my year,
Why don't we focus on others?
Why don't we look at the positives?
Why can't we be happy?

Thomas Chard (14)
Heolddu Comprehensive School, Bargoed

This Is Me

I am truthful
I have a theme for safety
I am hard-working

I am short and friendly
Some people call me crazy
I am determined and smart
And I have lots of generosity

I am made of jokes
Topped off with some loyalty
I take shelter under friends
And speak to them consciously

At my core, you will find
Someone who speaks truthfully
Someone who is outgoing and kind
This is me.

Kody Price (12)
Heolddu Comprehensive School, Bargoed

New School

When I first joined Heolddu,
it was mysterious to me
but with a laugh and a game
it turned rather fame.
With a bit of money and free time,
I can grab a baguette of mine,
they hold lots of fat but I don't regret it
because I'm not diabetic.
But something I do regret
is falling down the stairs and spraining my ankle,
that's not very merry.
With Harlee making me burst with laughter in English.

Ethanjay Harding (11)
Heolddu Comprehensive School, Bargoed

Sport

My name Alfie,
I like sport because sport is really good,
My favourite sport is rugby,
But I like football as well as rugby,
I like rugby better than football
Because rugby is more physical than football,
I like going out with my friends
To play games like hide-and-seek, tag,
Football and rugby and lots of other games,
Sometimes I will go to youth club on a Monday and Thursday,
My favourite food is pizza.

Alfie Cusack
Heolddu Comprehensive School, Bargoed

This Is Me

A gust of wind,
loyal to its storm,
respectful to its breeze.

A bird,
honest to its chick,
flying to its nest with ease.

A tree,
stuck to its Welsh roots,
and proud to do so,
with please.

Stay to your thriving roots like the tree,
but zoom and elevate like the bird
and soar like the wind.

A boy,
burning with passion,
but frozen with creativity.

Dewi Miles (12)
Heolddu Comprehensive School, Bargoed

This Is Me

Music gives me joy
I love it a lot
Like a kid with a toy
Live without it, I could not

Many types of genres
Many I have heard
It would be my honour
To make music for the world

Music is so good
It can get a bit wild
Like a fire and wood
But only certain styles

Instruments are fun to play
And learning too
It takes longer than a day
Learn one, should you?

George Holdsworth (13)
Heolddu Comprehensive School, Bargoed

This Is Me...

I have changed over time,
but all these traits have stayed by my side.
My intellect flows through my veins.
People who don't know me call me daring,
but the real ones only know me as caring.
My introverted soul stays at rest,
I try to find the words
but my confidence only flows into my heart,
but not to the rest.
I value myself but others more.
My empathy flows out of my core.

Niamh Higgs (11)
Heolddu Comprehensive School, Bargoed

This Is Me!

I am me.
I am annoying and I might be overdramatic but,
this is me!
Some people might think I am selfish and loud
but that's not me.
This is me!
At my core, you will find a kind, loving
and outgoing person.
I am caring, empathetic and attentive.
This is me!
These are the bricks that have built me
and if you don't like it, don't talk to me because
this is me!

Sophie Evans (12)
Heolddu Comprehensive School, Bargoed

This Is Me!

At my core, you will find that I'm very sporty.
I'm also very confident within sports.
I believe that I'm very helpful when people need it.
I'm random and fun.
I'm friendly and awesome
I'm funny and fair and I also care.
I'm very grateful and kind and I'm very creative with my mind.
I'm thoughtful and brave
I'm not shy, I will wave.

Zak Pearson (11)
Heolddu Comprehensive School, Bargoed

What's Important To Me

Family is for love
Family is for joy
Family is for kindness
Family is for commitment
Family is for the good times
Family is for the bad times
Family is for the memories
Family members go
Family member join
Family is for the loving support
Family is for the truth
Family has your back
Family is there for you when you're down
Family is forever.

Blake Price (14)
Heolddu Comprehensive School, Bargoed

That Is Me

Me is me and I am I
Happiness comes upon daily
No one thinks bad about me
Or do they?
Feelings come upon me in ways I don't want them to come
A big black cloud is around me on a bad day
I love the sun, the sun loves me
Warm sky makes me feel alive
That's me
Happiness is me
Full of energy that can get on people's nerves
But that's me.

Gethin Evesham (12)
Heolddu Comprehensive School, Bargoed

I Am Me

S hopping makes me happy
U nderwater animals make me wonder
M y passion is to be a vet
M y personality is kind
E njoying spending time with my friends
R eliable friend.

E njoying spending time with my family
L ove my family
L ove my friends
I love to dance
S now makes me feel good!

Summer Ellis (11)
Heolddu Comprehensive School, Bargoed

This Is Me

My walls are built of positivity that keeps me in line.
When I feel scared, I remember I am kind.
My core is full of honesty, which will never change.
If I look sad or blue, I feel strange.
I am made of loyalty just like a tree.
My roots are strong and courageous.
My branches are supportive and generous.
I am topped off with love and happiness for all, here or above.

Megan James (11)
Heolddu Comprehensive School, Bargoed

Who Am I

I am who I am,
I will be who I want to be,
I don't care what you think of me.

I am a summer baby,
I enjoy rugby and sports,
I have a dream to play for Wales,
And that dream is going to come true.

I like playing games,
I like playing with my friends,
I like practising my kicking for rugby,
I can't wait for what's ahead of me.

Ben Watkins (12)
Heolddu Comprehensive School, Bargoed

This Is Me!

This is me!
I am made of independence, confidence,
and that makes me, me.

I am unique and imaginative because this is me.
I take shelter under my kindness and empathy.
I thrive on helping others because that makes me, me!

I can be clumsy, reliable,
helpful and free.
Thoughtful, sporty, caring, honest and
these are the bricks that build me!

Lexie Derraven (12)
Heolddu Comprehensive School, Bargoed

For I Love Rugby

Being on that field in those moments,
Makes the voices fade,
The day I do not adore rugby,
Will never be a day,
For rugby is I,
And I am rugby,
For I love rugby,
And rugby loves I,
For it is fuel for infinite joy,
That will always be there,
When strife enters my life,
Rugby is by my side,
For rugby is my life,
And rugby makes I.

Alfie Hollifield (13)
Heolddu Comprehensive School, Bargoed

This Is Me

These are the bricks that built me
sporty, funny, friendly.
At my core, you will find
intelligent, brave, good friend.
I have a base of
energetic, positive, confident.
My walls are made of
thoughtful, respectful, helpful.
I take shelter under
pleasant, agreeable, sympathetic,
I am made of
joyful, supportive, humorous.

Jenson Griffiths (11)
Heolddu Comprehensive School, Bargoed

Football Heroes

F ootballs kicked around the field
O range sun shone on the pitch
O nly the best of the best can play
T rees grow around players
B alls kicked into the nets
A ll of the world chants as their team plays
L ong shots are taken, it's 50/50
L ord gifted everyone so we have a chance.

Lloyd Smith (11)
Heolddu Comprehensive School, Bargoed

Who Am I?

Who am I?
My name is Chloe,
My life is very crazy,
I have 6 sisters,
Which is quite a hassle
But I love them so it doesn't matter,
I have lots of pets,
I love them, they are the best,
I love my family and friends, they are so supportive,
My life is really the best,
I can't wait to see what's next.

Chloe Evans (11)
Heolddu Comprehensive School, Bargoed

This Is Me

People scare me,
But not all people,
Some people, I truly care for.

Sometimes, all I want is to be alone,
But other times, I want to be with my friends,
My friends are truly my favourite people.

People say I'm funny,
Even when I don't mean to be,
But I don't think I am,
Not one bit.

Peyton John (13)
Heolddu Comprehensive School, Bargoed

This Is Me

These are bricks that built me...
a good friend, loving and reflective.
I have a heart of honesty,
positivity and bravery.
I'm made of respect,
sensible and smart.
My walls are loving and humble.
At my core, you will find
strength, thoughtful and funny.
I will always be supportive,
nice and fast.

Reegan Thomas (11)
Heolddu Comprehensive School, Bargoed

This Is Me

T ender moments, shared and free
H eartbeats sync in unity
I ndividually, a cherished decree
S elf-discovery, the key

I nward paths, where I find glee
S elf-expression, authentically

M aking peace with what I see
E mbracing life, 'this is me'.

Coen Jones (14)
Heolddu Comprehensive School, Bargoed

This Is Me

I am me,
You are you.
I can be who I want to be.

Brave.
Smart.
Funny.

This is me.
People always see the best versions of us,
But is that really you?

Clumsy.
Drained.
Annoying.

This is also me,
Let people see you on the inside.
This is me.

Lola Heath (12)
Heolddu Comprehensive School, Bargoed

I Am Gracie

I   am Gracie Jenkins

A   very good friend
M   ature beyond my years

G   reedy (when it comes to pizza)
R   eliable and dependable
A   dog lover
C   onfident in different things
I   ntelligent and eager to learn
E   mpathetic and supportive.

Gracie Jenkins (12)
Heolddu Comprehensive School, Bargoed

Me

My structure is built on
Friends,
Sports,
And family.
I have three sports I may succeed,
Football, rugby and 100-metre sprint,
My idols are,
Louis-Rees-Zamit, Usain Bolt and Salah.
The place I belong
Is in Wales,
Where the grassy plains strive,
And it's where I lie.

Matthew Heywood (12)
Heolddu Comprehensive School, Bargoed

This Is Me!

This is me, a big and loud boy.
This is me, a gymnast that can fly.
This is me, a singer, not afraid.
This is me, a winner, who thinks they got it made.
This is me, emotional, from the start.
This is me, from the very start.
People come, people go.
This is me, a human, finding my home.

Oliver Stedman (11)
Heolddu Comprehensive School, Bargoed

This Is Me

The wild is a calm place to be
Can be silent as a mouse
Exploring can calm me
Outside can decrease stress
Without it, mental health would drop like flies
Nature is my relaxing area
But sometimes nature strikes with disasters
Which can affect us
But all you need to do is wait.

Kian Hurley (13)
Heolddu Comprehensive School, Bargoed

This Is Me

These are the bricks that built my life,
Concrete confidence and steel smarts.
I'd say my focus foiled my strife.
My all-round alertness isn't quite art.
Power's imperfect, prowess grants pride.
The quiet brick's cracking, almost
Broken, yet the wall has not died.

Jake Thomas (12)
Heolddu Comprehensive School, Bargoed

This Is Me

- **P** laying football is my therapy
- **H** aving a good game makes me happy
- **O** ver-exercising makes my body ache
- **E** xcitingly, I wait for my next football game
- **B** eating the opposite team gives me confidence
- **E** ventually, I will make it to be a pro footballer.

Phoebe Underwood (12)
Heolddu Comprehensive School, Bargoed

This Is Me

I am honest
And I'm not going to change
I am an introvert
But I'm not going to change
I am generous
And I'm not going to change
I am punctual
But I am not going to change
I may be all of these things, good or bad, but I won't change
This is me.

Aimee Thomas (12)
Heolddu Comprehensive School, Bargoed

This Is Me

Rugby makes me happy,
I love rugby,
Being on the field,
It's an unreal feeling,
There's nothing like it,
Everything goes away,
All the voices go away,
Rugby is forever in my heart,
It will last forever,
Rugby is my life,
It always will be.

Callum Charles (14)
Heolddu Comprehensive School, Bargoed

Netball

N o one passing the ball
E veryone running around the hall
T raining on a Friday night
B alls bouncing off the wall
A ll running up the hall
L aughing as they miss
L osers they are, we finally win.

Jesse Lewis (12)
Heolddu Comprehensive School, Bargoed

This Is Me!

I am determined,
I am dedicated,
I am focused.

There is no backing out,
no plan B,
or no stopping.

If it doesn't work,
make it work,
make it better,
make it the best.

Never stop,
never doubt,
never give in.

Reuben Smith (12)
Heolddu Comprehensive School, Bargoed

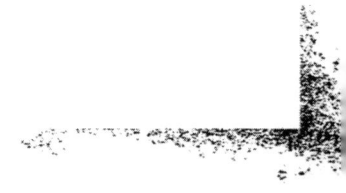

I Am Who I Am

This is me
Lucas Tamcken is the name
He was born for the fame
When he came out the womb
He lit up the room
Acting under the limelight is what he does
Acting is his buzz
Seeing himself on the TV is what he wants to see
Climbing up that legend tree.

Lucas Tamcken (14)
Heolddu Comprehensive School, Bargoed

This Is Me

A mbitious about most things new and old
L ooks forward to the future and the adventures that await
F inds things fun that I like to do
I nterested in school and the opportunities that it can give
E verything about me is unique.

Alfie Jones (13)
Heolddu Comprehensive School, Bargoed

This Is Me

S   is for studious, truly hardworking
A   is for ambitious, determination
R   is for resilient, my ability to bounce back
A   is for adventurous, willing to try something new
H   is for harmonious, a friendly and peaceful person.

Sarah Banks
Heolddu Comprehensive School, Bargoed

This Is Me

Before me was a field full of daffodils
A vast mountain with emerald hills
A ruby dragon flying proudly
As the sheep baa loudly

In a school far away
There was a child
Who wouldn't be swayed
But they're as quiet as a mouse.

Emily Zhu (13)
Heolddu Comprehensive School, Bargoed

Be Yourself

Hi, I'm Lexi,
And I'm twelve,
I've got something to say to you -
No matter what anyone says to you,
Please be yourself,
Even if you're shy,
Be yourself,
And please be kind to all,
And you are meant to be yourself.

Lexi-Joanne McMahon (12)
Heolddu Comprehensive School, Bargoed

If I Could Make A Friend

One cup of kindness,
A teaspoon of loyalty,
A sprinkle of love and laughter,
After all that, we need to add...
100ml of manners and confidence,
90g of intelligence and style,
With a big fat smile,
Then mix it all up
In one big cup.

Ava Williams (13)
Heolddu Comprehensive School, Bargoed

I Am Me

I am Lexie, I am me,
I try my best to make sure I succeed,
I am bright, I am kind,
I have a bubbly personality,
Art and netball are my priorities,
My friends and family are important to me,
Shopping is what I love,
This is me.

Lexie Pascoe (10)
Heolddu Comprehensive School, Bargoed

Year For Freedom

It's been a year since it happened,
It's been a year since police came,
It's been a year since I was violated,
It's been a year since he was arrested,
It's been a year since he died,
It's been a year of freedom.

Maisie Harrison (14)
Heolddu Comprehensive School, Bargoed

Me And I

A ll I think about is my friends and family, but I think about them because they mean a lot to me.
L oving my family and music, I always feel happy with both, I also feel happy with my cat, GG.
L ife can be stressful.

Allise Yuile (11)
Heolddu Comprehensive School, Bargoed

This Is Me

At my core, you
will find I am
fair and funny
but keep in
mind, I am
kind.
I am loyal,
thoughtful,
loving
and grateful,
and if you
ever need
help, never
fail to come to
me.

Evie Carver (11)
Heolddu Comprehensive School, Bargoed

Harry

- **H** oping one day to go pro in scootering
- **A** t one point, I'll go pro scootering
- **R** iding a Santa Cruz V10
- **R** iding my scooter proficiently
- **Y** elling loudly after coming 1st in a competition.

Harry Allison (10)
Heolddu Comprehensive School, Bargoed

This Is Me

I am filled with love alone
Loyal and kind at the bone.
Behind me, you will see that I'm
As stubborn as can be.
Helpful and reliable,
Lazy and clumsy.
These are the things that make me, me!

Niamh Eynon (12)
Heolddu Comprehensive School, Bargoed

This Is Me!

At my core, you will find
a loving friend who'll be by your side.
My base is made of a positive mind.
My empathy fills my heart with care,
for others, I will always be there.
This is me!

Neve O'Callaghan (11)
Heolddu Comprehensive School, Bargoed

This Is Me

I'm built as a brick because I was made to be one
I am sarcastic because I'm funny and I make people laugh
I have a base of a house because they are solid and they can't fall down.

Connor James (10)
Heolddu Comprehensive School, Bargoed

This Is Me

I am joyful,
I can be crazy,
I can be clumsy,
this is me!

I am smart,
I am creative,
I am honest,
this is me!

These are the bricks that build me.

Lloyd James (12)
Heolddu Comprehensive School, Bargoed

This Is Me

In my core, you will find someone who is grateful and patient,
Although, on the outside, I may seem quiet or just friendly,
But inside, this is me,
So that is who I'm going to be!

George Hamod (11)
Heolddu Comprehensive School, Bargoed

Willow

W onderful walks
I ce cream in the sun
L ollipops from the shop
L ucky to be here
O ctopuses through the sea
W ales is my country

Willow Farrell (11)
Heolddu Comprehensive School, Bargoed

This Is Me

I am a tree standing tall,
my roots buried in Wales,
my branches are made of kindness, respect,
confidence and independence.

This is who I am.
This is me.

Kian Christensen (12)
Heolddu Comprehensive School, Bargoed

Football

Never back down,
Practise and always try your hardest,
And always chase your goals,
Try the hardest you can try,
Keep working for it,
Reach the top.

Jacob Davies (11)
Heolddu Comprehensive School, Bargoed

I

I struggle to concentrate,
I struggle to comment.
I struggle to realise what's right and wrong,
I struggle to see what's real or not.

Lily Gardner (13)
Heolddu Comprehensive School, Bargoed

All About Me In A Recipe

Add a spoonful of happiness,
Now a cup full of generosity and stir well,
Now add a dash of confidence and love,
Now some clumsiness.

Kaylyn Woodward (12)
Heolddu Comprehensive School, Bargoed

I Am Black

I am black
That, I have always known
But where I'm from
That never seemed to show

Because everyone there is black
No need for discrimination
At home, skin colour
Has no definition

The only things regarded are
The entirety of your values
What you stand up for
What makes you, you

So what about now
That I'm living in another place?
Where different people abide with
Those of a different race

We have the White, the Asian
The Mixed, the Black
Is there a race that is at the front?
Is there one that's at the back?

I need to know if I fit into your meaning
Of my specific race

Do I act like I'm black?
Or am I out of place?

Does *BLACK* stand for
Brilliant, Loving, Amazing
Creative and Kind?

Because that's what it means to me
It describes who I am
It keeps me true
Hopefully, not just to myself
But also to you.

Ire Ajimuda (16)
John Willmott School, Sutton Coldfield

The Ginger Boy

In a world where dreams take flight,
there's a ginger boy with eyes so bright,
tall and strong with a heart of gold,
in the realm of football, his story unfolds.

With fiery red hair that matches the sun's rays,
he conquers the field in his noon way.
With every kick and every stride,
he wears his passion like a badge of pride.

His green eyes sparkle with determination,
a vision of strength and no hesitation.
In the gym, he trains with all his might,
chasing his dreams to soar to the great height.

In this tale of a ginger boy so fine,
the world witnesses his star brightly shine.
With every goal, he sets hearts aglow,
a hero in the making, watch him grow.

Dylan Trowman (16)
John Willmott School, Sutton Coldfield

Can It Be My Reality?

Along the sanctity of life, I seek the essence of finding me...
Out there amongst others, pretending to be something that they cannot possibly be;
Is it possible for me to turn all my childhood dreams into reality
While also being labelled as a black sheep?

Me, myself and I wonder if in 100 years, my name will be engraved into history.
Even when all odds stack against me, I will turn dreams into reality.
Fuelled by sheer will and fright of not fulfilling my destiny.
I'll show why the rest are not like me and show why I'm known as the black sheep.

Quayumm Oluwa (16)
John Willmott School, Sutton Coldfield

Is This Really Me?

Is this me?
The person in the mirror
They look brave
And I feel afraid
Am I them, or is it an illusion?

Is this me?
The person in the mirror
They look strong
And I feel weak
Am I them, or is it all a lie?

Throughout my life, I've been told to believe in myself,
However, we are put down
And led to believe we aren't good enough
When we should all believe
I am that person in the mirror!

Melissa Hayden (15)
John Willmott School, Sutton Coldfield

Who Am I?

Who am I?

Am I a daughter?
Am I a daughter who shimmers in her parents' glow?
Or am I a daughter who wants to be free like a sparrow gliding in the breeze?

Am I a friend?
Am I a friend who holds her friend's hand in the dark?
Or am I a friend who wants to be propped up by an arrow?

Am I a teenager?
Am I a teenager who is as neat as a freshly trimmed haircut?
Or am I a teenager whose room looks like it has just been burgled?

Am I a sister?
Am I a sister who is an umbrella in the rain to her sister?
Or am I a sister who's irate and is not a doormat?

Am I a granddaughter?
Am I a granddaughter who gets bonnes notes scolaires?
Or am I a granddaughter who is a phone-aholic?

I am me.
I am a girl who gets good grades.
I am a girl who spends loads of time on her phone.
I am a girl who is responsible.

I am a supportive sister but have anger
I am a girl who is messy and doesn't care.
I am a supportive friend but I also want to be supported.
I am a girl who does want to please her parents.
I am a girl who also wants to have fun.
I am me.

Eloise King (14)
Kimbolton School, Kimbolton

Did They Really Make Me Any Different?

Time, time, ticks, ticks,
Did they really make me any different?

He was left with one
When he was still young
And he was still dumb
He blamed the tragic on old magic
Thinking it would bring him peace
But it did nothing to cease the pain of the loss
After all, what's a son without a mother?
He lost his father much later but was he really prepared?
We will never be sure, but know that really he cared

Though those before may have struggled
And I know I will too
I also know what brings together me and you
Time, time, ticks, ticks,
Did they really make me any different?

She was still a young woman
Yet she was not happy where she was
Her treasure taken, she was shaken
She left
423 miles away is a long way from home
A maid's job will do

But life's better when there's two
Love is compelling
He loved her and she loved him too
So getting married down in old Galway was the right thing to do
We learn from those who pass and those who came before
That happiness can be eventually found on Ireland's old shores

Time, time, ticks, ticks,
Did they really make me any different?
Learning about their lives and stories is exhilarant
The clock works improved and it's unlike it was before

Though those before may have struggled
And I know I will too
I also know that love is what brings together me and you
Love
Although love is different and it may come with pain
Their lives did continue life's beautiful chain.

Poppy Todd Boutou (13)
Kimbolton School, Kimbolton

This Is Me

As I read your introduction, I couldn't help
But feel inspired to write a poem about me.

So, here it is!
I, oh so bright,
A young girl with a heart of light,
As the sun rises up to the sky,
I'm up and ready to give it a try.

Looking in the mirror, you see
A reflection of who I'm meant to be,
A human, but not just any,
I, it's me, or am I who you see?

What makes me, you may ask?
It's my kind heart and my bright mind,
And my determination to always be kind,

So now I've found to realize, it's like a charm,
I look around and there's no harm,

So go on, I hear inside, *You can shine your light,*
Wherever you are, even out of sight.
Embrace each day with all your might,
For you are destined to do things right,
So fly up high, I dare you to try,
And spread your wings into the sky.

Amina Benzait (11)
La Retraite RC Girls' School, Clapham Park

I Am Who I Say I Am

My name is Pison, and I am 12.
I have two brothers who go by the names Nabiel and Elhanan,
My brothers, in my eyes, are young men,
If you have seen my mum, you would believe that she is the kindest and most innocent person you can see.
And that is by guarantee.
My dad is so kind and works for most of his day to get some food on the table and any added stuff we want and need.
I have known him to always to succeed,
I am very thankful for my family, friends and all the people in my life,
I thank the Lord for the love he has given me in my life.
I have been to a variety of places such as Brighton, Ethiopia, and Bognor Regis.
My parents have work that is prestigious,
My friends are loyal, fearless and passionate.
I owe so much to my teachers and family, and they are so compassionate,
Loyalty is the key to everything.
I want to be like Martin Luther King,
I have milk chocolate skin and I am proud of it,
I like to knit.
I am Eritrean and you will probably not know it, but I do not mind, I am unique in that way and many more,

Always go hardcore,
And never show your weakness.

My name is Pison and that is unique, nobody can take that away from me.
I am born on the 20/10/2011 and some people do not like it but that is fine by me.
If you have known me, I could be funny but serious at times.
My favourite slogan is 'education for a lifetime',
I am who I say I am,
You may not like it but that is fine by me.
I am who I say I am,
I will not force you to like my way but at least be respectful,
I am beautiful in my own way, in a style that I believe is slay,
You do not have to like it but who cares when I am in my own world!
You may not like my style,
But I am who I say I am.

Pison Mulugeta (12)
La Retraite RC Girls' School, Clapham Park

This Is Me

I do not care what people say about me,
Since I am who I am meant to be, nothing can prevent me,
Listen to this poem and soon you will see
The way I live in reality,
I live with one brother and sister, everyday it is World War 3,
Going on journeys with my family is so chaotic, you wouldn't believe me,
My favoured sport is football, enjoying the victory,
Going on tournaments with my teammates is what makes it neat,
My first weeks of high school have been most precious to me,
Making new friends along my journey,
I was born in Manchester, with most of my family living there,
I visit frequently, but trust me the journey is not the best quality,
Islam is my religion, preaches good deeds,
Mercy and kindness, to the right path it leads,
Upon all humanity, God showers his grace,
Regardless of colour, nationality or race,
I am a Muslim and God I praise,
For all his blessings, my voice I raise,
In one God I believe, no equal has he,
Lord of everything, compassionate to me,

This is what I believe,
I give charity daily to help those in need,
In turn, it gives me fulfilment and countless deserving rewards,
To myself, I'm as certain as can be
That all of us, to some degree,
Have qualities that even we don't see,
I ponder what I'm yet to learn about the person I am and yet to be,
I'm here in the moment,
That's all I could be,
And that's all I can say,
This is me!

Imaan Javid (11)
La Retraite RC Girls' School, Clapham Park

This Is Me

I looked at the vast green field and the breeze flew through my hair.
I have copper curls that grew, that wrapped round my glittery brown skin.
This is me, it is who I want to be, and who I am.
I sat in my class, daydreaming about my country.
I dream of the day that I sit by the sea, my feet sinking into the white sandy beaches and dreaming of what could be.
I see flying fish by the shore. I want more.
This is me and is where I want to be.
I am looking at my parents, my mum's smooth dark brown skin shimmering as she floats in the water,
my dad's milky skin getting tanned and he is bobbing along in the water.
This is us, it is all we can ever be.
Some tell me I am not. I say, say what you want, it doesn't matter to me at the end of the day.
You're annoying, you're a liar.
I say at least I don't eat green eggs and ham and my pants aren't on fire.
This is me, trying to put me down, but I bob up like a spring up, down, up, down.
You're half, you're weird.
I put up a fight, put me down, I get back up and say all you want.

I am Irish.
I am Bajon.
I am Welsh.
I am Scottish.
My eyes illuminate the sky and you could plant flowers in my heart.
I am me and it is all I can ever be.

Nila Connors (11)
La Retraite RC Girls' School, Clapham Park

This Is Me, You Are You

I am Hosanna
This is me
I am Eritrean
This is me
I like being me
This is me

I am me
You are you
You have your own opinions
I do too
I'm lots of fun, caring and kind
But on some occasions, I can be mean malicious, scary and unkind
I learn from my mistakes, I can admit
I am human like everyone else
This is me, I'm like no one else

I like people and like to have fun
But sometimes, I want to be alone just with no one
I have feelings and so do you

So, we shouldn't judge what people are going through
I know, I know people don't believe that's true
But you should go in other people's shoes and be honest with yourself now that is true!
We are human we can't hide, so let's stand together and show some pride!

This is me a sister, a daughter, a friend you can rely on
A girl who is being the best friend, who you can cry on
An ordinary girl who can get things right or wrong but no matter what, she stands confident and strong
I know this because the truth never hides
I'm worth something and so are you

This is me, who are you?

Hosanna Samson (11)
La Retraite RC Girls' School, Clapham Park

This Is Me

When you look in the mirror what do you see?
A girl, a boy, or do you see me?
Not me, but you!
So what do you see?

A depressed soul who needs healing,
Or a young child who hates school,
And feels like everyone thinks she's a fool?
A perfectionist with anxiety and maybe even ADHD?
But deep down, it's who God wants me to be,
Embrace it! Own it! Love it!
Because this is me!

No, I can't,
But help me!
I know, my child, just believe.
But what? How? No, I can't leave my family!
Fear not, as they are already with me.
What about my dad, he doesn't live with me?
I know, I know but that is not your problem,
For one day I will see you on Judgement Day
And we will rejoice,

So believe.
Thank you, Lord, you have freed me.

So Kaira, your faith in God has set you free,
So that's the end of that,
Because Yahweh is within me.

Kaira-Siti Hawley (11)
La Retraite RC Girls' School, Clapham Park

This Is Me

I am Hannah, I am Hannah
I am summer and bright
Full of sun
I am one-of-a-kind
That makes me unique
I am Nigeran and Ugandan
I love food
That's just part of me
I like jollof rice and chicken; it's crispy too!
I am kind and caring
But people call me a heading
This shows how I am!
Who I am?
I am fearless and brave
No one can come between
I am open and ready
For anything to come
Nothing can stop me from being myself
I am good at maths
So please don't nag
I love to dance
I love music
My favorite type is Afrobeat

My people are very confident
Just like me
Which is one of my special abilities.

Hannah Odeh (11)
La Retraite RC Girls' School, Clapham Park

I Love My Life

I love my life!
Do I, do I really, or am I just acting?
No, I do!
I am not pretending nor acting
I love my life! I am not pranking!

I am from Trinidad (my mother's side)
I am from Jamaica (my father's side)
But I am from England... which blows my mind

I learnt that when you are young, you need to treasure it
Because no one stays young forever! So be sure to measure it
When you are an adult, you miss that time of being a baby
In your mother's hand, clinging to her, and her thinking maybe
Never wanting to let go, never really wanting to know
Where my journey of life will go
But one thing I know for sure
I love my life!

Des'shaniea Stephenson-King (11)
La Retraite RC Girls' School, Clapham Park

This Is Me

I belong to my country,
I belong to my race,
People walk around and see I'm not afraid,
I belong to my culture, my religion, my faith,
I praise the Lord and pray for forgiveness every day,
I belong on the court, your score is none,
Because I'm tall, I play basketball,
That's where I belong and also at school,
That's my second home, to educate and learn more,
5, 6 years, it's been a long journey,
Either way, they'll all remember my story,
My mum and dad will be so proud,
They'll sit up there upon their cloud and say out loud,
"This is my child, what a great mind!"

Mitcheka Jackson (11)
La Retraite RC Girls' School, Clapham Park

Enjoy My Life

I may have difficulties in life behind my smiling face,
But sometimes you just have to appreciate life.
Even though it's hard or I may struggle,
You will never see me fail.
Take a breath and breathe
In the world,
Take a moment to appreciate
How wonderful it is.

We all have wonderful moments,
But life isn't equivalent.
It is just like an instrument,
Life is a present,
It has constant movement.
My life can be deranged,
But I won't let that stop me from enjoying my life.

Enjoy life and don't waste it...

Elyona Adonis Opoku (12)
La Retraite RC Girls' School, Clapham Park

This Is Me

From my head to my toes,
from my looks to my clothes,
this is me.

From my body to my soul, all the way to my mind,
I know I can sometimes be a bit too eager to thrive,
this is me.

Sometimes I need help,
sometimes I feel independent,
with me being my own lock
to my own key.
This is me.

I know I am worth it.
I know I belong.
Whatever I do, I can learn a lesson or two.
But being myself means I am not trying to be like somebody else.
This poem is all about me, as you can see.
This is me.

Jessica-Ria Miyanda (11)
La Retraite RC Girls' School, Clapham Park

This Is Me

I love my old friends.
They are wonderful friends.
They may be far,
But my new friends are stars,
And I'm loving my life so far.
Primary school is in the past,
Secondary school is the new.

All my friends who I once knew
Are fading away in the blue.
But treasured deep inside my heart,
Are friends both old and new.
Oh, how really I wish they knew,
How much I miss my old crew.
But know that I am saying,
That this is who I am.
And who I'll always be.
This is the me,
That I hope you now see.

Maria Iloba (12)
La Retraite RC Girls' School, Clapham Park

Me

My name
My name means weaver
To weave a path the fates want
My fabulous name

My name means power
I am a ruler of elves
Elven wisdom in my name

My name means warrior
A defender of mankind
Honing my inner strength

My name means the wit
Charm and the spices of life
Willows in my veins

My name is my voice
My power, my strength, my pride
My names are special
Penelope Aubrey Alejandro Sales.

Penelope Aubrey Sales (11)
La Retraite RC Girls' School, Clapham Park

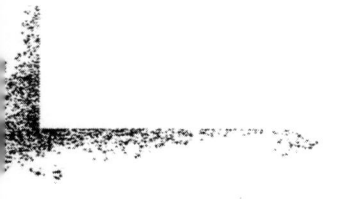

This Is Me

This is me
This is me
I have different features
I am unique

I might not look like you
You might not look like me
But we are different people
No one can compete

You might be bad at Maths
And good at Science
But that's just you
Their words are lifeless

So the next time you compare yourself
Just know that
They are them
And
You
Are
You.

Aicha Cisse (11)
La Retraite RC Girls' School, Clapham Park

This Is Me

T his is me
H er/she is my pronoun
I am an ambitious, proud, and positive girl who likes to draw
S mart I am, but be careful because I can get fierce easily

I nteresting I am, with differences from other people
S ad I can be sometimes, but that's the same for everyone

M yself is always me, so
E xcellent I am, but remember that this is me.

Christianah Ajanaku (11)
La Retraite RC Girls' School, Clapham Park

This Is Me

Temi is what they call me
But Temidire is how they know me

I am a Nigerian
If you don't believe me
Just ask my guardian

Dark, black and beautiful
My ancestors who are wonderful
Taught me how to express myself and be thankful

As my name is translated
We learn the real surprise
Mine has turned into blessings
That is where the truth lies.

Temidire Adejuwon (11)
La Retraite RC Girls' School, Clapham Park

I Am Me And I Like Me

I am me,
And I like me,
I am me, I smile, not frown,
I love, not hate,
I am special,
I am glad I have the eyes I have and the hair, the skin colour,
I am love and hope,
I am brave,
I am courageous,
I am pretty and smart,
I like PE and maths,
I am a child becoming an adult,
I am me and that feels just right.

Eguono Ehwenomare (11)
La Retraite RC Girls' School, Clapham Park

Pisces Sinking

A pair of twin goldfish
Flapping their fins like paper fans
They venture deeper and deeper into the dark blue
Skin turning into glass
Tentacles sprouting from their organs
Wrapping their exterior, forced into a sphere
Now they can only tumble, stumble, fumble
As they slowly sink into the uncertain
And as they sink, they...
No, not they

She. She lost sight of her sister
The golden sunlight at the break of dawn
The bubbles of laughter exploding with glee
The one holding the headlights of their path
The blanket fort hiding the stairway to the top bunk was no more
Young girlhood gone along with her memories
In a suitcase awaiting a new adventure
She was surprised by how she could summon
The oceans that the plane flew past
Right onto her cheeks,
Running
Down
In
Droplets.

The goldfish turned jellyfish sank deeper
Finding solace in the cold darkness
Because she thought
As long as she's making friends with monsters in the dark
No one would see her deformity
The half of a breathing heart
Exposed and raw and where itshould not be
The other half of her
The good half, lost to time
And the current half
The new whole.
Missing a whole lot of the past
The K51 to school
The 36th floor wait up the elevator
The castle kindergarten
My shared bunk beds
My grandparents' place every Saturday
Watching my shadow slowly take up space
Made her mark
And now nothing at all.

My tentacles hug me closer
Stinging myself with my own poison
Signalling the end of my adolescence
In a foreign land 5962 miles away
I laid the other half of me to rest.

In the casket, a crystal jellyfish
With faded crayon
A heart drawn on wonkily
A child and their last best efforts...

Nevaeh Kwan (17)
New College Pontefract, Pontefract

This Is Me

Embedded within each cell of
my body lies a dominating force.
One of great energy, coruscating like the sun itself.
A limitless source of power containing
the ability to expel detriment
or create an omnibenevolent being.
It is a force that lies within us all, however
it is through our true nature
that we choose how to harness this power.
The power that I possess
reverberates restlessly,
yearning for a desire to experience
Eudaimonia.
To cherish the beauty nature
possesses.
To harness the ardent longing for
ultimate love
and share it with the world.

Kimberley Eglen (16)
New College Pontefract, Pontefract

Polychrome

I am a canvas,
stained with the hues of past, present, and future strangers.

I cannot show you the ochre brush strokes
that have been left by conversations about sunsets,
or the violet freckles from those about the moon.

I cannot show you the constellations of grey-tinted greens
from every cat I have met in the street, and stopped to pet;
I cannot show you the navy smudges, painted layer upon layer
each time I slow to let a pigeon walk across my path.

I cannot show you the cobalt fingerprints pressed
by a friend's appreciation of my naivety,
nor are you able to see the designs of alizarin, etched gently
by a care shown during nocturnal vulnerabilities,
in summers that have since passed.

I cannot show you the blotted spots of silver
from the things I have tried to erase,
or the way in which they still shimmer
softly when they are held in a certain light.
I cannot show you the still-blank spirals,
which I have taped over, reserved
for the shades of those whom I hope will sketch
masterpieces.

And if you were to ask me my favourite colour, I could not tell you:
I could only describe to you the pattern each has left on my skin.

Lilian Fanthorpe (16)
New College Pontefract, Pontefract

My Saviour, The Moon

Running.
Along the pavement,
down the alleyways,
up the hills,
behind the buildings,
above the motorway.

Every turn that presented itself,
I grabbed by the hand
and let it drag me, batter me, beat me
but I was nowhere near finished,
throwing myself from right to left,
exhausting.
The streets keep me hostage.
My feet slam upon the pavement below,
I feel the rhythmic vibrations from head to toe.
Grasping at any avenue that would grant me freedom from this journey.
This unfathomable run.

My legs heavy.
My soul heavy.
Panting,
breaking,
crumbling.

Then, dusk.
The moon finally revealed itself to me
and freed me from my running,
my debt.
But I know, when the sun appears and comes out of its hiding place,
even if it's concealed by clouds,
my running will continue,
the moon can only do so much.

I'll run until I die.

Belle Needham (17)
New College Pontefract, Pontefract

Mirabellier - Dead Wood, Coryneum Blight, Rust

I wish I had new flesh
Seeping you into my skin
All of you!
Like candlewax
Melt you
Pour you over my arms
And drizzle
And bask!
I'm honeycomb

Break me up. Eat me:
Runny, thinned, honey-like
Oil and oil
I'm soupy wax
Non-newtonian
Crack my shell and pierce
The egg's skin - outpour
The seeds
The warm breath of iron

Tarmac lung, O, I call
Name me
Rotten. Bleachy, bloated

Pink. Blotchy. Handful of my
Skin shavings both coarse and tender
Alight
Break me up! Radio signal again
Sour fizzing frequency
Delicious - Dégoûtant!
Crasseux and nauseating
Wouldn't have it any other way.

I told you to eat me
Though, don't -
Maybe sip
I'll give you indigestion
For consumption unmoderated.

Kairos Ford (17)
New College Pontefract, Pontefract

This Is Me

My life
My life may be different to yours
But we are still similar in some ways
Whilst you celebrate Christmas with jingle bells
The planes start to propel
When your snow falls
My ocean reels in its iridescent spell
With sun so hazy it makes you melt
Whilst you're meeting family from faraway lands
Over some pints near the pine tree
When it's so cold you hear the fire crackle in a beat
All I hear is the barbecue rattle, sizzling the meat.

Jasmine Gibson (16)
New College Pontefract, Pontefract

This Is Me

Hair like fire,
The child of Satan.
Eyes like the ocean,
Drowning in tears.
Marks of the sun,
Dressing my cheeks.
But who am I?

A lover of music,
And songs known all too well.
Life is too delicate
To not stake claim on what's mine.
As my tears ricochet,
I am yet to find peace and the answer:
Who am I?

Harriet Marris (16)
New College Pontefract, Pontefract

Dying My Hair

A haiku

Auburn was the hair
That has been dyed a light blonde
Now I want it back.

Aimee Smith (16)
New College Pontefract, Pontefract

Tired

Laugh, run, play, and weep
Man, I just wanna sleep
I get up in the morning
When all I want to do is continue snoring
This is what I feel every time
Then I see the morning sun, but I guess I'm feeling fine
I wake up but not in my mind
I wake up but not in my mind
I wake up but not in my mind
I wake up but not in my mind
I roll over, half asleep
Tired as hell, but I keep
Moving on with my day
Wake up and pray
Praying that everything will be okay
Why can't I go chill on the bay?
I just lie back down but the alarm starts to beep
Goddamn it, why can't I just sleep?

Jake Offord (14)
Seadown School, Worthing

The Cars And Me

T he cars go past fast
H ow peaceful it is watching them
I am feeling bored
S o I continue staring out the window

I s this really what I want to do?
S ometimes, I want to see something happen to the cars

M y mind is still bored
E very car I see, it makes me less bored.

Josh Willis (14)
Seadown School, Worthing

Post Mort

P erhaps I'm crazy
O r not
S ometimes I might scare people
T hough I don't mind

M aybe they don't understand
O r they might not like it
R igor mortis
T ired, so tired.

Faye Bowles (12)
Seadown School, Worthing

Family

F   unny, laugh and jokes
A   ngry, mum and dad
M   emory of the past
I   nteresting, everything about them
L   ove my family
Y   ou are fantastic.

Kai Jardine (16)
Seadown School, Worthing

The Things I Like

T rains and trampolines
H orses
I ce cream
S lides

I like football
S wimming

M usic
E lephants.

Jonty (7)
Seadown School, Worthing

This Is Me

This is me
Mmmmm... this is me!
You will need some things to find the key and no, it's not easy.
Somewhere in this world,
There is a hidden potion...
You will need mystical objects of different proportions.

Yes,
Unusual items, you might say,
Just have a look at the list and you will fall in dismay.
I am full of a complex range, from knowledge to crime,
From being a nerd to sometimes being late on time.

Here they are,
56g of madness and 1kg of fun,
1 ton of fulfilment and a 10kg brain that could make you stun.
However, I am not too old nor am I too young,
Add those up altogether and now you know my weight.

So, I guess this is me,
But here you have everything in order to find the key.
In your hands, you have the hidden potion,
Just mix those foods of different proportions...

Keshav Bansal (12)
The Commonweal School, Swindon

Silent

Silent like awkward silence.
Silent like a house at night.
Silent like a concentrating class.
Silent like a library.
Silent like mute.
Silent like the trapped.
Silent like the upset.
Silent like a predator stalking prey.
Yet within the silence
There is always a whisper
A murmur
A giggle
But I do not
Whisper or murmur or giggle.
I am silent.
I am silent when reading.
I am silent when drawing.
I am silent in class.
I am silent with anyone.
I am the quiet kid called Bekah.

Bekah Ashdown (12)
The Commonweal School, Swindon

This Is Me

A sunshine on a cloudy day,
The rainbow after the storm,
The one who helps,
The glue keeping everything when it's about to fall apart,
This is half of me,
The one who stays home alone,
The one who gets angry easily,
Not many people know this side of me,
It's kept hidden, within a rage monster,
Ready to strike at any known moment,
But whichever side, this is still me, the ordinary 12-year-old.
This is me.
The furious rage ball who bangs the drums,
The extrovert who is always happy to talk!

Ariadne Uphill
The Commonweal School, Swindon

One Life, All Lives

I was always the weird one
Always on the outside plate
Was I bad? No
I was not filled with hate
I was always strange
I never wanted to change

I was always fearful
Scared of all
But I lost my plateful
And I grew tall

Sometimes you do not like you
Sometimes you feel alone
But we can grow anew
And become known

So, now this is all over
Unlucky like a three-leaf clover
But humans have the right to be
And this is me.

Georgina Mercer (12)
The Commonweal School, Swindon

This Is Me

Hi, I'm Evie and I am really friendly
I have a lot of hope
It is very dope
Every day I walk to school
Every day I look so cool
This is me
I'm Evie
Hanging out with my friends, knowing all the latest trends
I am very social
Have so many friends in total
I'm amazing in every way
This is me
I'm Evie.

Evie Wischhusen (11)
The Commonweal School, Swindon

I Am Lola

I am Lola
Lola with the flaming red hair
Lola with the muddy brown eyes
Lola with the soft pale skin
People will read between the lines
And rewrite them in words they see fit
They'd rather make me their own
Than understand who I truly am
But no one knows what is within
So I refuse to be rewritten in their stories
Because I know I'm not just what they see.

Lola Alderson (12)
The Commonweal School, Swindon

All Over The Place

Just me
                                                                    Doing random
                        Me things
That are
                        Quite normal
                                                                    Eh mostly?
Not mostly.
                        Extremely normal
Me things
    That are by no means ambiguous or all over the place.
Did I
                                                                  Fool you?
                        Just me
                        Doing random
Me things
                                                                 Will only
                                                                 Ever be
All over
                        The place.

Christina Paterson (12)
The Commonweal School, Swindon

This Is Me

I am proud,
I am loud,
I am meant to be,
I am me,

I try,
I cry,
I am meant to be,
I am me,

I am kind,
I use the power of mind,
I am meant to be,
I am me,

I am alive,
I am proud of my life,
I am meant to be,
I am me.

Emily Pidduck
The Commonweal School, Swindon

All About Me

This is me
This is my poem
This is my explanation
I am kind
I am playful
I am really easy to talk to
I am like a rabbit, really fluffy
I am very easygoing
This is my poem
All about me.

Alice Poole (11)
The Commonweal School, Swindon

YoungWriters
Est. 1991

YOUNG WRITERS INFORMATION

We hope you have enjoyed reading this book – and that you will continue to in the coming years.

If you're the parent or family member of an enthusiastic poet or story writer, do visit our website **www.youngwriters.co.uk/subscribe** and sign up to receive news, competitions, writing challenges and tips, activities and much, much more! There's lots to keep budding writers motivated!

If you would like to order further copies of this book, or any of our other titles, then please give us a call or order via your online account.

Young Writers
Remus House
Coltsfoot Drive
Peterborough
PE2 9BF
(01733) 890066
info@youngwriters.co.uk

YoungWritersUK YoungWritersCW
youngwriterscw youngwriterscw

SCAN THE QR CODE TO WATCH THE THIS IS ME VIDEO!